D0929300

# LIFE ON THE
# PLAINS

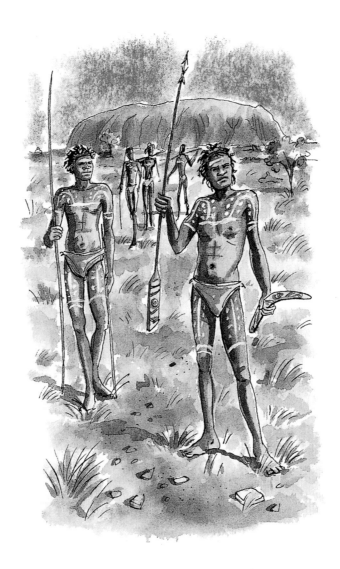

Written by **Catherine Bradley**

World Book Ecology

Published in the United States and Canada by
World Book, Inc.
233 N. Michigan Avenue
Suite 2000
Chicago, IL 60601
in association with Two-Can Publishing

© Two-Can Publishing, 2001

**For information on other World Book products, call 1-800-WORLDBK (967-5325),
or visit us at our Web site at http://www.worldbook.com**

ISBN: 0-7166-5230-7 (Life on the Plains)
LC: 2001091764

Printed in China

1 2 3 4 5 6 7 8 9 10 05 04 03 02 01

Photographic credits:
p.4-5 ZEFA/K. Bonath p.7 (top) Bruce Coleman/Andy Purcell (bottom) Bruce Coleman/Michael Freeman p.8 (top right and bottom left) Bruce Coleman/Gerald Cubitt p.9 Bruce Coleman/Peter Ward p.10 Bruce Coleman/Jane Burton p.11 Survival Anglia/J.B. Davidson p.12 (top right) Survival Anglia/Cindy Buxton (bottom left) Survival Anglia/Jen & Des Bartlett p.13 (top right) Ardea, London/Clem Haagner (bottom) ZEFA/Horus p.14 Bruce Coleman/Hans Reinhard p.15 (top right) Bruce Coleman/Norman Myers (bottom) Bruce Coleman/Gunter Ziesler p.16 Bruce Coleman/Dr Eckart Pott p.17 Planet Earth/Jonathon Scott p.18 Bruce Coleman/L.C. Marigo p.19 ZEFA/Leidman p.20 Hutchison Library/Dr Nigel Smith p.21 (top right) Bruce Coleman/Mark N. Boulton (bottom) Bruce Coleman/D. Houston p.22 Survival Anglia/Richard & Julia Kemp p.23 Bruce Coleman/Simon Trevor

Front cover: Bruce Coleman/R.I.M. Campbell Back cover: NHPA/Peter Johnson

Illustrations by Michaela Stewart. Story by Claire Watts. Edited by Monica Byles.

# CONTENTS

All words marked in **bold** can be found in the glossary.

# LOOKING AT THE PLAINS

Most of the world's plains are flat grasslands, with only a few trees to break up the landscape. Most of them stretch, like a shimmering ocean, as far as the eye can see.

In the cooler parts of the world, people have farmed the plains since early times. The rich **soil** provides most of the world's food harvests. Today, the plains are often broken up by fences that mark out different fields. Plains are used to grow crops like wheat, oats, and barley, or to provide food for raising grazing animals, such as cattle and sheep.

The grasslands of Africa are home to a variety of wildlife. Many species feast on the grasses, and are hunted by **predators**. Lions, elephants, and zebras are hunted by people. People have also turned much of the animals' territory into farmland. These wild animals are now confined to the few remaining areas of unspoiled plains.

▼ Trees on the **tropical** plains have thick bark to protect them against fires, and deep roots to tap underground water. Many have spikes to defend their leaves against grazing animals.

# WHERE IN THE WORLD?

Most plains lie toward the center of the Earth's continents. Often they are located on the inner side of high mountain ranges, and so they are cut off from the sea winds that bring rain. The lack of rain means that there are no great forests on the Earth's plains, because most trees need a lot of water to grow.

The tropical plains lie in belts of hot land on either side of the **Equator**. They do not have seasons such as summer and winter. Instead, they have dry and wet periods.

**Temperate** grasslands lie farther away from the Equator and are hot or cold depending on the seasons.

Different places have different names for their plains. In Russia, the plains are called **steppes**. In North America, the grasslands are called **prairies**, meaning meadows. The plains of South Africa are called **veld**, which is Dutch for field. In Africa and Australia, the grasslands are known as **savannahs**. The people of South America call their plains the **pampas** and the **campo**.

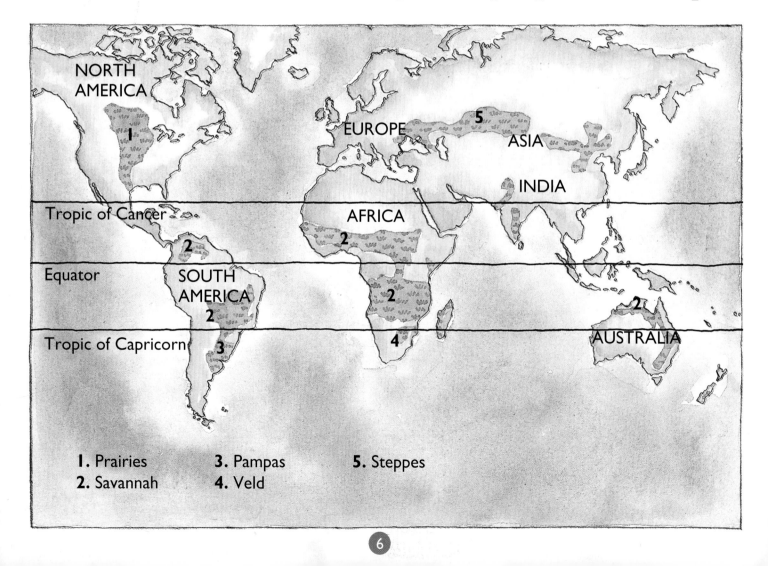

**1.** Prairies    **3.** Pampas    **5.** Steppes
**2.** Savannah    **4.** Veld

◄ A combine harvester works its way through a field of ripe wheat in England. The blades cut, or reap, the stalks, then they shake, or thresh, the ears to release the valuable grains.

▼ In Southeast Asia many of the plains are flooded to grow rice, the main food eaten by about half the people in the world. Most of the back-breaking work is still done by hand. This woman from Java is transplanting rice.

# PLANTS ON THE PLAINS

Grasses dominate the world's plains. There are about 8,000 species in all, covering about one-quarter of the Earth's surface. They grow well on the open plains because they need a great deal of light. They can survive drought, being trampled, very hot sunlight, fire, and frost. If there is not enough water or heat, they just stop growing until conditions improve. Antarctica is the only area in the world where grasses cannot thrive.

In cooler regions, the grasses tend to remain short. In the tropical grasslands, however, they can grow to enormous heights.

Among the grasses may grow plants such as dandelions, daisies, and clover. Plants that grow from bulbs, such as lilies, also thrive on the plains.

▲ The plains grasses have many uses. In South Africa, a Cape weaver bird perches above its nest. The male has carefully woven the bell-shaped nest from dried grasses to attract a female. The female will approve the nest, then prepare an inside lining to cushion the eggs.

◄ A swollen baobab tree rises from a sisal plantation in Madagascar. The spongy trunk stores rainwater, then shrinks in dry weather. In a drought, elephants have been known to tear off branches to reach the water hidden inside.

▶ A tumbleweed rolls around a dusty plain in Mexico. These plants develop rounded tops, then wither and break away from the ground during fall. The large, light plant then rolls around the plains, tossed about by the winds. As the weed tumbles, it scatters its seeds over a wide area. Tumbleweeds are considered a nuisance by farmers because they often pile up against fences and fill up small valleys.

# FOOD FACTS

● Grass seeds are lightweight and easily carried by the wind. They soon colonize a patch of bare ground, sending out a network of underground stems, which sprout new leaves. Farmers have learned to breed certain varieties to provide plentiful and cheap food crops.

● Some grasses are used to feed farm animals. The farmer may sow a mixture of two or three kinds of grass seed together with clover. In summer, the grass may be cut to make food that will be stored to feed the animals in the winter.

● **Cereals** are grasses that provide food for people. Varieties include oats, maize, wheat, barley, millet, and rice. Popcorn, cornflakes, and corn oil are made from corn. Wheat grains are ground into flour for bread and pasta. Oatmeal is made from oats.

# ANIMAL LIFE

In the wild, the plains grasses feed huge herds of **grazers**. Most grazers are **herbivores**. A great variety lives in Africa, including antelopes, giraffes, rhinoceroses, elephants, and zebras. Many of these animals prefer to browse on the trees and bushes. Giraffes feed on the lower branches of the acacia, so these thorny trees end up looking like umbrellas.

Grass leaves and seeds also feed hordes of insects, such as butterflies and grasshoppers. The soil below is tunneled and heaped up by termites, or ants. One huge African anthill even had a village built on it!

The south American pampas is home to small grazers such as the mara and cavies, wild relations of the guinea pig. Larger animals, such as kangaroos and wallabies, feed on the savannahs of Australia.

▲ A dung beetle tests a rabbit pellet. These beetles often roll the droppings of elephants and other large animals into smaller balls, then bury them. They lay their eggs in the dung, which provides food for their larvae.

▶ On many of the world's plains, the main protection from predators is to run fast. Some animals live in herds, like these African zebra drinking at a waterhole, so that there are plenty of eyes and ears to spot danger. A lion could be lurking behind any nearby bush.

## ANIMAL ANTICS

The South American anteater has a specially shaped snout for digging up ants, termites, and grubs from the soil. It has a long whip-like tongue, which it uses to catch the insects.

Prairie dogs, or marmots, live in North America. They burrow tunnels to house their big communities, or "towns." One town was thought to have held up to 400 million prairie dogs.

# BIRDS IN THE BUSH

Birds of many different shapes and sizes live on the plains. Clouds of small birds feast on the plentiful seeds and vast numbers of insects.

The African savannah is ruled by the meat-eating vultures. They circle above the plains in search of dead flesh. Marabou storks and ravens also join in the **scavenging**. Eagles and hawks also hunt prey on the plains.

Several flightless birds, such as the South American rhea and the Australian emu, roam the grasslands. These birds are fast runners and tend to be large. The African ostrich can grow to nearly 8 feet (2.4 m) tall. The birds live in flocks and feed on seeds, plants, and even small animals.

▲ Cattle egrets live in Africa near antelope, cattle, and elephants. They perch on an animal's back to eat insects, such as lice or ticks, living there. Egrets warn their hosts of any danger by flying off suddenly.

◄ Two ostriches look after their young. At one month old, the babies can run as fast as an adult – up to 40 miles (64 km) per hour. The ostrich can live up to 70 years and is the world's largest living bird. It has good eyesight to spot its enemies and can kick an attacker to death using the sharp nails on the two toes on each foot.

▶ An African secretary bird stamps on a grasshopper. It eats insects, frogs, lizards, small tortoises, and snakes. Sometimes it flies high, drops its prey, then lands and eats it.

▼ Huge flocks of small birds, such as these pink cockatoos from Australia, swoop over the grassy plains. The cockatoos feed mainly on a variety of insects, fruit, nuts, and grass seeds.

# HUNTERS OF THE PLAINS

The best-known African plains dwellers are the hunter cats, such as lions. Lions live in groups, or prides, of up to 30 animals in a territory. They eat mainly wildebeest, zebras, and gazelles. Other African hunters include cheetahs, leopards, hyenas, and jackals.

On the Russian steppes and the prairies of North America the grey wolf was once a mighty hunter. It is now very rare, having been nearly wiped out because of its threat to farm animals and people. In North America, the coyote is now the main predator.

The main hunter on the pampas of South America is the cunning jaguar. It will lie in ambush and stalk for long periods to catch its prey.

## SNAKE CHARMER

The mongoose is a slim animal, similar to a ferret. Some species are famous for killing snakes. The mongoose has sharp eyesight and can usually dodge a snake's fangs. It also eats insects, rats, snails, worms, and lizards. Some will smash eggs and eat them, too.

◄ The flecked coat of a cheetah **camouflages** it against the sun-dappled grasses. Cheetahs are the fastest short-distance runners of all land animals. They can sprint at 68 miles (110 km) per hour. They hunt mainly during the day for antelopes and gazelles.

Cheetahs are now rare, because many of their old hunting grounds have been turned into farmland. They have also been hunted for their **pelts**. Most cheetahs live in Africa.

► **Carrion** is left by an animal once it has eaten its fill. The scavengers then gather to share the spoils. Here, spotted hyenas and vultures pick a skeleton clean on an African plain. In the background, a solitary marabou stork waits patiently for its turn at the feast.

Scavenging birds often have featherless, bare skin on their necks and heads to help them feed more easily inside the dead animal's body.

▼ A zebra runs for its life, fleeing from a lioness. Often several lionesses will surround their prey so that it cannot escape. When it is killed, the male lions and cubs come to share the meal. Lions have few enemies, and sleep up to 20 hours a day.

# CROSSING THE PLAINS

Many of the grazing herds of the plains travel enormous distances in search of food. The wildebeest of the East African plains **migrate** every year in search of fresh feeding grounds in the river valleys. At the beginning of the dry season, the separate herds gather to start the long trek. They are often joined by groups of gazelles and zebras. The immense herds will travel up to 125 miles (200 km) and will often mate on the way. When the rainy season begins, they return to the open plains, where their calves will be born.

Saiga antelopes on the vast Russian steppes also ramble over very long distances in search of fresh food and water. They are known to travel up to 220 miles (350 km) across the steppes in a single year.

▶ The best-known migration on the East African plains is that of the wildebeest. They travel in enormous groups of up to 1,000 animals. The lengthy journey is often very dangerous, especially when crossing a rushing river. Many animals do not survive.

▼ On the North American prairies, bison used to migrate yearly, but they are now confined mainly to **national parks**.

# PLAINS PEOPLES

The first people are thought to have lived on the plains around 40,000 years ago. They hunted animals and ate berries and roots. Gradually, the people learned to tame some animals and to harvest food crops from some of the plants. Soon, they developed ways of breeding plants and animals to create new ones from wild varieties.

Today, food crops for humans and animals are grown in vast fields all over the world. A range of different animals are kept on the pastures for their meat, milk, or skins.

In many lands, some people live on the plains as **nomads**. They usually keep herds of animals and move from place to place in search of grazing land. On the steppes of Asia, for example, the Mongols and Kazakhs keep herds of cattle, sheep, and horses. The animals provide these people with food, clothing, and the materials to make tents.

▼ Wealthy farmers use cowboys to ranch cattle on the Mato Grosso plain of South America. The cowboys work on horseback and wear tough leather clothes to protect them from thorns as they ride across the plain.

► A young Masai warrior practices a traditional dance. The Masai live on the borders of Kenya and Tanzania in East Africa. They build villages near a water supply and move on when the grass of the surrounding land has been eaten by their cattle. They mainly feed on cow's blood mixed with milk, as well as a few vegetables, traded from other tribes for meat and skins.

## PEOPLE FACTS

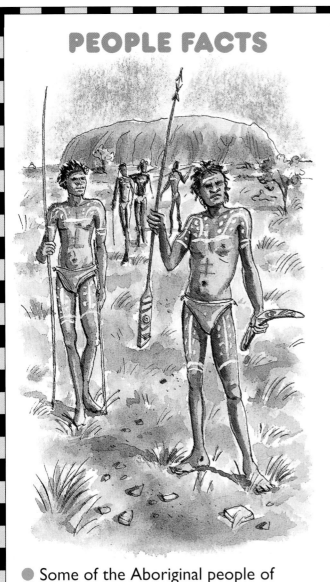

● Some of the Aboriginal people of Australia still live by hunting animals and eating wild plants. Most now live in nature **preserves**. In the past, Aborigines would remember long-distance routes across country by learning complex songs that mentioned important landmarks.

# PLAIN DESTRUCTION

People have greatly changed the world's plains. Long ago in the northern **hemisphere**, people cleared forests and plowed up the grasses to make farmland. In Britain, 80 percent of the forests were cut down. The wild plants and animals were replaced with domestic crops and herds.

Modern farmers use chemicals, such as fertilizers and pesticides, to help their crops grow better. Some of these chemicals have ruined the soil and even damaged water supplies. Overfarming also leads to **erosion**, or soil being blown or washed away.

On the tropical plains, people have also used the best land for farming. Some farmers have allowed herds to overgraze the grass, again causing erosion. The grass roots hold soil in place, but with grass and soil gone, only bare rock remains and the hungry animals will move on.

## DID YOU KNOW?

● Millions of bison used to roam the North American prairies. Overhunted, they now survive mainly in nature preserves.

● Prairie dogs only occupy areas already overgrazed by livestock.

● Saiga antelope once covered the Russian steppes. Few survive today.

▲ A man proudly displays the hide of a jaguar. These rare animals are hunted for their high-quality fur, which is made into clothes and shoes. Other plains animals that have been hunted close to **extinction** just to provide luxury products, include the rhinoceros, the lion, and the elephant. Many countries around the world now ban the import of any goods made from endangered animals.

▶ Bare soil shows through in Masai country, Kenya. Here, the herds of sheep and goats have been allowed to overgraze. Where the grass has gone, soil quickly blows away. In hot countries such as Kenya, the ruined plains may soon turn into desert.

▼ Fires occur naturally on the African plains in the hot, dry season. Local trees have thick bark to protect them from the heat. The charred grasses soon grow back from the roots. Some fires harm animals and destroy crops.

# SAVE THE PLAINS

Of all the people in the world, farmers can help most to save the plains. They can try to use chemical fertilizers more carefully so that the soil is not damaged. They can plant trees and hedges to prevent soil erosion from the wind. If any land has been overgrazed, they can fence it off to prevent animals from damaging it even further.

Farmland on plains at the edge of deserts should be **irrigated** to make the best use of water supplies. Crops that are specially adapted to the dry conditions should be grown. Every few years, farmers should leave parts of their land unfarmed so that the soil can recover its richness.

The wild animals of the plains also need protection. In Africa, many elephants have been killed for their **ivory** tusks, while the spotted cats are gunned down by **poachers** for their pelts. Most of the countries where the African elephant lives keep these animals in national parks and set up armed patrols to protect them. People should refuse to buy products made from ivory and animal fur to stop the trade.

▼ Giraffes must watch out for predators. They sleep for only about 20 minutes each night, divided into three or four short naps. Another greater threat today comes from humans who kill giraffes for their skins and turn their grassland homes into farms.

▼ Large areas of Africa have been set aside for wild animals to live in peace. However, the rhinoceros is still hunted secretly by poachers. There are not very many of these animals left on the plains of Africa today. Rhinos graze on grass, twigs, and leaves. White egrets eat the insects that live on rhinos, as well as those turned up in the soil as the rhinos walk along.

# PLAIN PERSUASION

### Support campaigns
There are many groups trying to stop the killing of plains wildlife. They need money and support to continue. Watch for news on television, the radio, the internet, newspapers, and magazines for information on such groups.

### Stop the trade
Explain to people why you would not wear fur clothes, or buy products made from rare species.

# RED LEAF AND THE GREAT BUFFALO BULL

*For thousands of years, people have told stories about the world around them. Often, these stories try to explain something that people do not understand, such as how the world began. This story, told by a Plains Indian tribe, tries to explain how the group of stars we know as the Pleiades came to be.*

Long ago, a girl named Red Leaf lived in a teepee on the plains with her seven adopted brothers. Every day, six of the brothers would go out hunting, while the youngest, who was known as Little Brother, would stay behind to chop wood and fetch water. Red Leaf cooked the meat that the brothers brought home, and made and mended their moccasins and clothes. They all took care of each other and were very happy.

One day, six of the brothers went hunting, and Little Brother went to fetch water, leaving Red Leaf alone in the camp. On Little Brother's return, he found Red Leaf gone, and there were signs of a struggle. from the hoofprints, Little Brother knew that the Great Buffalo Bull, who ruled over all the buffalo, had stolen Red Leaf.

When his brothers returned, Little Brother told them his story. All the brothers were afraid of the Great Buffalo Bull, but they knew they must save their precious sister.

The seven brothers built a series of four strong corrals, one inside the other, so that they would have a safe place to run to if they managed to bring back Red Leaf. Little Brother went out and collected anthills in his cloak. He sprinkled them in a steady line, all along the ground inside of the innermost corral.

Then, taking up their very special magic medicine sacks, the seven brothers bravely set off, following the dusty trail of the Great Buffalo Bull's enormous hoofprints.

They travelled for a long time. At last, they came to a hill overlooking the vast plain. Below them, covering the plain as far as they could see, stretched the buffalo herd. Right in the middle was a wide open space, where the Great Buffalo Bull stood, with poor Red Leaf lying nearby.

"We must get a message to Red Leaf, to tell her we are here, " said the oldest brother. He brought out his magic medicine sack, which was made from the skin of a blackbird. As he held it in his hand, it turned into a living blackbird and flew off into the center of the herd, right to the place where Red Leaf lay.

But before the blackbird could deliver the message, it heard the Great Buffalo Bull bellow furiously: "Get away, spy!"

The earth shook, as the Great Buffalo Bull pawed the ground, and the blackbird flew off in fear.

The second brother took out his coyote skin medicine sack. As he held it, it turned into a living coyote, which set off boldly through the buffalo herd until it managed to reach the very place where little Red Leaf lay.

"Get away, spy!" roared the Great Buffalo Bull in a terrible fury, and the cowardly coyote swiftly turned and ran away.

The third brother's medicine sack was made from the skin of a little yellow bird. The bird was so tiny that it reached Red Leaf without the Great Buffalo Bull noticing.

"Red Leaf," whispered the bird, in its tiny voice. "Pull your cloak over your head and wait for your seven brothers to rescue you."

When the little yellow bird returned, Little Brother took out his gopher skin medicine sack. As he placed the skin on the ground, it turned into a living gopher and began to dig right under the herd. Little Brother followed the gopher along its tunnel and came up under Red Leaf's cloak. He led her down the tunnel, leaving her cloak over the hole. Then Red Leaf and her brothers ran as fast as they could to the corrals.

It was not long before the Great Buffalo Bull noticed something was amiss. He pushed Red Leaf's cloak aside with his hoof and discovered the secret tunnel below. Bellowing furiously, he charged off at once in the direction of the brothers' camp, with the rest of the herd hard on his heels. In no time at all, the Great Buffalo Bull was standing outside the corral with his whole herd gathered around him.

"Give me back my Red Leaf!" roared the Great Buffalo Bull.

Inside the corral, the brothers and their sister trembled with fear.

The Great Buffalo Bull began to charge the first corral. Soon, the logs lay scattered at his feet.

"Give me back my Red Leaf," he bellowed again.

"Let me go to him and the rest of you will be spared," brave Red Leaf begged her brothers.

But Little Brother insisted that they would all be safe and sound.

It was not long before the Great Buffalo Bull had tossed aside the logs of the next three corrals. But when he came to the line of anthills, he found that every grain of sand had turned into a huge rock. The whole herd charged at these from every side, until it seemed that they would surely reach Red Leaf and the seven brothers, who quaked inside.

"Have no fear," said Little Brother, as he shot an arrow into the sky. A tree appeared, reaching skywards.

Little Brother helped his sister climb into the branches and the other six brothers followed.

As Little Brother swung himself last into the tree, the Great Buffalo Bull broke through the anthills. He charged at the tree, taking huge chunks out of its trunk. Each piece the bull tore off immediately joined up again, and the tree remained as good as new.

As for Red Leaf and her seven brothers, they kept climbing the tree until they reached the sky. And you can still see them there. Red Leaf is the main star, and Little Brother is the smallest one, over to one side.

# TRUE OR FALSE?

*Which of these sentences are true and which ones are false?*
*If you have read this book carefully, you will know the answers.*

1. Tropical lands have spring, summer, fall, and winter.

2. A small mongoose can catch and kill a snake.

3. Popcorn, cornflakes, and corn oil are made from barley.

4. Prairie dogs live in a network of tunnels called a town.

5. South American cowboys wear clothes made from woven grasses.

6. There are about one million species of grass in the world.

7. Giraffes will sleep for up to 14 hours every day.

8. The ostrich can live up to 70 years.

9. A swarm of locusts can rapidly devour enough food to feed 400 thousand people for one year.

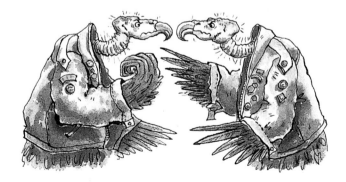

10. Scavenging birds, such as vultures, often have bare skin on their heads.

# GLOSSARY

● **Camouflage** hides an animal against its surroundings to protect it from predators, and can help it to capture prey.

● The **campo** is the tropical grassland in South America.

● **Carrion** is dead flesh.

● **Cereals** are grasses that have been developed by people to provide food.

● The **Equator** is the imaginary line round the Earth, halfway between the North and the South Poles.

● **Erosion** is the wearing away of soil or rock by wind, rain and floods, ice or frost.

● **Extinction** occurs when the last of an animal or plant species dies out. This often happens when animals are overhunted by people or other species, or when they lose their food or feeding place.

● **Grazers** are animals that feed on grasses or other plants.

● A **hemisphere** is one half of the Earth. There are two halves: the northern and the southern hemispheres.

● **Herbivores** eat only grass and other plants. They have special teeth with ridged surfaces to grind the grass into small pieces.

● To **irrigate** is to artificially water land that naturally tends to be dry. Water is often channelled through ditches.

● **Ivory** is what the tusks of elephants, and some other animals, are made from. It was once used to make piano keys.

● To **migrate** means to move from one area to another. This often takes place once a year as the seasons change and animals and birds look for fresh supplies of food and a warmer climate.

● **National parks** are large areas of land protected by law, where the landscape cannot be changed and the birds and animals cannot be harmed by hunters or collectors.

● **Nomads** are people who move from place to place following animal herds, which provide them with food and materials to make clothes and tents.

● **Pampas** are the temperate grasslands of South America. Pampa is the Spanish word for plain.

● **Pelts** are the skins or furs of animals.

● **Poachers** are people who kill animals illegally to make money from selling their meat, skins, horns, tusks, or other parts.

● **Prairies** are the temperate grasslands of North America.

● **Predators** are animals that hunt and kill other animals.

● **Preserves** are special areas set aside under the laws of a country for certain people or animals to live in.

● **Savannahs** are the tropical grasslands in Africa, South America, and Australia.

● **Scavenging** is when animals or birds feed on the remains of animals that they have not hunted for themselves.

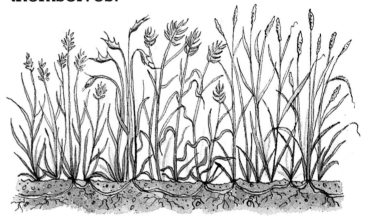

● **Soil** is the top layer of ground in which plants grow. It is made up of ground-down particles of rock.

● The **steppes** are the temperate grasslands of both southeast Europe and Asia.

● **Temperate** describes the mild climate that is found in lands on either side of the tropical area.

● **Tropical** describes the hot climate around the Equator.

● **Veld** is the temperate grassland of South Africa.

# INDEX

# RESOURCES

**Friends in the Wild,** by the editors of *World Book Encyclopedia* and *Childcraft*, 1998. This book focuses on the animals of grasslands and other environments.

**Northern Prairie Biological Resources,**
http://www.npwrc.usgs.gov/resource/resource.htm
Information about plants and animals of the northern plains of the United States and prairie provinces of Canada.

**One Day in the Prairie,** by Jean Craighead George, 1996. Prairie ecology is explored in text and black and white drawings.

**The Smithsonian Guides to Natural America–The Northern Plains–Minnesota, North Dakota, South Dakota,** by Lansing Shepard and Tom Bean, 1996. Dozens of full-color photographs and maps document the breathtaking natural wonders of America's Northern Plains, from Minnesota's boundary waters to the badlands of the Dakotas. Describes a wide range of wildlife refuges, national and state parks, and other nature areas.

**What Do We Know About Grasslands?** by Brian J. Knapp and Mark Franklin, 1992. This book is part of a series that shows children ages 9-12 how to care for different types of environments.